The Kingfisher Book of

SOCCER SKILLS

From warmup to final whistle—
the essential guide

KINGFISHER
LONDON & NEW YORK

Copyright © Kingfisher 2012
Published in the United States by Kingfisher,
175 Fifth Ave., New York, NY 10010
Kingfisher is an imprint of Macmillan Children's Books, London.
All rights reserved.

Distributed in the U.S. and Canada by Macmillan, 175 Fifth Ave., New York, NY 10010

Library of Congress Cataloging-in-Publication data has been applied for.

Created for Kingfisher by Tall Tree Ltd.
Photography by Michael Wicks

With thanks to Martin McMahon, Nick Allpress, Neal McLoughlin, Chris Mattey,
Martin Elcox, California F.C., and the Eversley Sports Association

ISBN: 978-0-7534-6873-9

Kingfisher books are available for special promotions and premiums.
For details contact: Special Markets Department, Macmillan,
175 Fifth Avenue, New York, NY 10010.

For more information, please visit www.kingfisherbooks.com

Printed in China
1 3 5 7 9 8 6 4 2
1TR/0112/WKT/UG/140MA

The Kingfisher Book of

SOCCER SKILLS

From warmup to final whistle—
the essential guide

CLIVE GIFFORD

KINGFISHER
NEW YORK

Contents

The beautiful game

Brazilian soccer legend Pelé once described the sport as "the beautiful game." Games can be exciting and dramatic. They can contain moments of bravery, controversy, great skill, and action. Two teams of players battle to keep possession of the ball, attack their opponents' end of the field, and try to score a goal.

Goals win games, but teams need to defend in order to stop goals from being scored against them and to win back the ball. When in possession of the ball, players can use any part of their body except their hands and arms to control and move the ball or to pass it to a teammate.

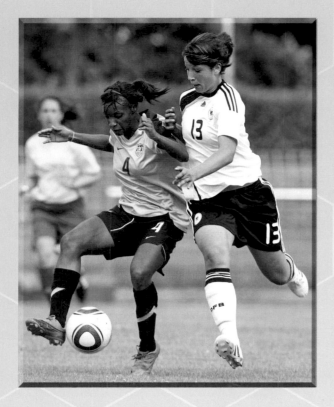

Germany's Sylvia Arnold (right) challenges the U.S.A.'s Crystal Dunn during an international game. The very best players get the chance to represent their country at different tournaments.

> "Football [soccer] is simple, but the hardest thing there is, is to play simple football [soccer]."
>
> Johan Cruyff

Children in the city of Niamey in Niger use a street as a makeshift soccer field. Because soccer is a simple game that needs little equipment, millions of people in all parts of the world play casual games every day.

Many ancient civilizations, including the Egyptians and the Chinese, played games in which players kicked a ball. Association soccer (the modern version of the game, which is called "football" in other parts of the world) has its historic home in England, however, where the first rules were drawn up in the 1800s. Since then, soccer has been exported all over the world to become the most popular team sport on the planet.

Wayne Rooney scores with a spectacular overhead kick during a game between his team, Manchester United, and local rival, Manchester City.

Players battle it out in a street soccer game during the 1700s. Soccer developed from these unruly mob soccer games into a global sport.

Players celebrate a goal scored by one of their teammates. Although the player may have conjured up a moment of magic to score, teamwork from the other players on his team created the opportunity to score.

The field

The field is where heroes are made, goals are scored, and games are won and lost. Unlike most other sports, a soccer field can vary in size. A full-size field is 295–394 ft. (90–120m) long and up to 295 ft. (90m) wide. Fields for professional games are usually covered with grass, although artificial fields are found in some stadiums.

The best soccer players often look exhausted at the end of a game—players may have to run 6–8 mi. (10–12km) during a game. Play stops only if the referee blows the whistle for a foul or other infringement or if the ball goes out of bounds from the field.

This goalkeeper takes a goal kick from the front of her goal area. Goal kicks are awarded when the ball crosses the goal line and was touched last by an attacking player. If a defending player touches the ball last, a corner kick is awarded.

A defender trips and fouls an attacker inside the penalty area. A serious foul, which prevents a possible goal-scoring chance, results in a penalty kick being awarded to the attacking team (see page 46).

AILTON
32

B.SUK

Goal line

Goal area

Goalkeepers are the only players who can touch the ball with their hands and arms, but they must be inside of their own penalty area. This keeper has handled the ball outside of his area, and the opposing team will be awarded a free kick (see page 44).

The ball stays in play even when part of it crosses a sideline or goal line.

The ball must completely cross a line to go out of play. If it goes off the side of the field, then the game will be restarted with a throw-in (see page 42).

An attacking player blasts a free kick past a wall of defensive players and at the goal. A full-size goal is made up of a net attached to two posts and a crossbar. The goal measures 24 ft. (7.32m) wide and 8 ft. (2.44m) high.

Penalty area

Center circle

Penalty spot

Center spot

Midfield, or halfway, line

Sideline (touchline)

Each half of the game is started with one team taking a kickoff from the middle of the center circle. The first touch must move the ball into the opponent's half, and the opposition team must stay outside of the center circle until it is made. Kickoffs are also used to restart the game after a goal.

Corner arc

A player takes a corner kick, aiming to cross the ball into the other team's penalty area in order for his teammates to try and score. The ball must be played from inside of the small corner arc.

PROFESSIONAL: soccer in which the players are paid a full-time salary to play

Soccer terms

Preparing to play

Leaping up high to head a ball one minute and sprinting hard or lunging for the ball the next— soccer puts your body under a lot of strain throughout a game. You should prepare your body and mind for the effort by performing a thorough warmup and muscle-stretching routine before you play.

Your footwear is by far the most important part of your equipment. Ignore cleats endorsed by star players in favor of ones that fit your feet the best, feel comfortable, and offer good support around your ankles. Many good cleats feature soft leather uppers so that your foot can "feel" the ball. Clean and dry your cleats after each game so they will last for a long time.

These soccer cleats feature screw-in studs to provide plenty of grip on a soft, wet field. Make sure all studs are tightened before play. Other types of cleats have molded bumps or textures for use on dry, hard ground and artificial turf.

Tie your shoelaces securely in a double knot, making sure that the lace ends do not trail on the ground.

A coach shows players how to stretch their hamstring muscles at the backs of their legs. All stretches should be performed smoothly. Never jerk or bounce into a stretch or perform them halfheartedly.

Players jog on the spot and perform high knee lifts, raising their knees so that their upper thighs are parallel to the ground. Tracksuits may be worn to stay warm before a game.

A long-haired soccer player ties her hair back before beginning a training session. Players must also remove any jewelry before they start playing.

If you get a few minutes on the field before a game, check out wind and weather conditions and make some passes with teammates to get a feel for the speed of the field.

PRO TIPS

Warming up can involve jogging and other activities that raise your heart rate and get your blood pumping faster around your body. Stretching muscles helps prevent minor muscle aches or more serious tears and injuries and improves your flexibility, too. Ask your coach to take you through a thorough stretching routine.

Shinguards protect the bony front parts of your lower legs from painful kicks during tackling. Many also have padding around the ankle and heel areas for added protection. Shinguards are secured with Velcro and socks are pulled up over them.

"Failure to prepare. Prepare to fail."

Roy Keane, ex-Manchester United and Ireland midfielder

FLEXIBILITY: the amount you can move your joints and body parts

Soccer terms

First touch

The ball will zip, fly, and bounce toward you at a great variety of speeds, heights, and angles during a game. How quickly, smoothly, and accurately you are able to control it with your first touch will determine how successful your next move is. You can use any part of your body, aside from your hands and arms, to control the ball. You can either cushion the ball's speed or use its pace to make a short pass or run with the ball.

Most of the time, you will want to slow the ball down on arrival so that you can get it under control near your feet in order to run, pass, or shoot. Players cushion the ball by withdrawing the body part that connects with the ball as it arrives. By moving their foot, thigh, or chest along the same path as the ball's, they can slow its pace so that it does not bounce out of their control.

A player controls a high ball using his chest. As the ball arrives, he leans back to cushion the ball's impact. His feet have a wide stance, and his arms are out to help him balance. The ball should drop gently in front of his feet, ready to be controlled on the ground.

Practice cushioning the ball with the side and instep (where the shoelaces are) of both feet. A player who can control the ball equally well with both feet offers a greater threat to the opposing team.

PRO TIPS

Control does not always have to be cushioned. Here, a player thrusts his chest out on impact to send the ball a short distance forward to a teammate. This is an example of firm control.

While most headers (see page 18) use firm control, a cushioned header will bring the ball down or can be used to make a short pass to a nearby teammate. The secret is to draw your head back as the ball arrives to slow down much of its pace.

The side of the foot can be used to control a bouncing ball or one that is rolling across the ground. This player has turned her receiving foot to contact the inside of the cleat with the ball. The foot is then pulled back as the ball arrives.

To cushion a falling ball with the top of your thigh, raise your upper leg so that it is almost parallel with the ground. As the ball arrives, drop your knee and pull your leg back and down so that the ball is cushioned and drops in front of you.

A good first touch takes a lot of practice. Work on your first touch and ball control whenever you can. Get a friend to pass the ball to you at different heights and speeds or use a wall to bounce the ball off if you're on your own. Concentrate on being balanced and watching the ball so that you can bring it under control as quickly as possible.

"When your first touch is good, it always gives you time to see the next situation."

Rafael van der Vaart, Dutch attacking midfielder

To outwit an opponent, this player has let a pass run across in front of his body rather than controlling the ball right away. He turns sharply to move in the direction of the ball's path, using its pace to leave the opponent behind.

Soccer terms   **CUSHIONING**: slowing down the path of the ball using a part of the body

Passing

Passing moves the ball between teammates, and slick, accurate passing can propel the ball around the field much faster than by running with it. A team that passes well is more likely to split defenses and create goal-scoring opportunities. Passes can vary in force and distance, from short flicks to long passes that cross the field. They can also be made with different parts of your feet.

You can use the outside of your foot to make a short flick pass by twisting your foot sharply at the ankle. This is a useful, quick pass to a teammate standing a short distance away.

The instep of your cleat (where the shoelaces are) can be used to connect with the ball to make both short and long passes.

1

To make a sidefoot pass, place your nonkicking foot to the side of the ball and turn your ankle so that the inside of your kicking foot faces the ball.

2

Swing your leg forward through the ball. Aim to make contact with the center of the ball—this keeps it low for your teammate to control easily.

3

As the ball moves away, your foot should follow through in the direction that the ball is heading. Try to keep your body over the ball during the pass.

With a lot of practice, you will be able to judge how much force you need to strike the ball to make a pass. This is known as the weight of the pass. Too much weight, and the pass will be difficult to control. Too little weight, and it might not reach your teammate. You can adjust the weight of your pass by pulling your kicking foot back a longer or shorter distance and striking the ball with more or less force.

Four players practice their short passing in a two-on-two game played inside a small, coned-off area. One pair tries to make as many passes as possible without the other pair intercepting a pass or the ball traveling out of the area.

★ *Masterclass* ★

Cesc Fabregas

The talented midfielder is a renowned passer of the ball with both feet, able to play short passes to keep possession or play a well-timed attacking ball to make a goal. It was Fabregas's pinpoint pass to teammate Andrés Iniesta that produced the winning goal for Spain in the 2010 World Cup final against the Netherlands.

"If you want to make it as a footballer [soccer player], you probably need to be practicing simple side foot passing every single day."

Gary Neville, ex-Manchester United and England defender

Pass placement is crucial. This player has aimed the ball a short distance ahead of his teammate so that he can sprint toward the ball and behind the opposition player. Learning when to make a pass and the best place to aim the ball only comes from practice and experience.

To make an instep drive, plant your nonkicking foot beside the ball and keep your body weight over the ball as you swing your kicking foot back.

Point your kicking foot down as you swing forward. Aim to strike the center of the ball with your shoelaces.

Keeping your eyes on the ball throughout, let your kicking leg follow through smoothly. The ball should fly toward its target.

Advanced passing

Aside from building a large range of passes to use, the most crucial element of developing your passing skills is to learn to pass well with both feet. Every soccer player starts out with a weaker foot. The secret is to work extra hard on that foot to bring it up to the level of your stronger foot. A soccer player who relies on one foot is much easier to play against because defenders know their opponent can only play the ball on one side of his or her body.

A lofted drive relies on similar technique to a regular instep drive. You create the extra height on the ball by leaning back a little as you strike the bottom half of the ball with your instep.

To make a chip pass, use a short, stabbing movement of your instep down on the bottom of the ball.

Your cleat acts like a wedge. The ball should rise sharply into the air, with little follow through.

Most of the time you will want to keep the ball low so that it speeds across the field's surface, but there are times when you want to send the ball higher. A chip pass can send the ball steeply up and over an opponent. A lofted drive is a strong strike of the ball used for making crosses into the opponent's penalty area or to send the ball a long way out of your own penalty area.

This attacker (in white) places his body between the ball and an opponent to protect the ball, before playing it to a teammate.

★ Masterclass ★

Steven Gerrard

Liverpool and England midfielder Steven Gerrard plays a trademark long pass to launch an attack. Gerrard is highly skilled at picking out teammates with both long- and short-range passes. He also uses the instep drive as a powerful shooting weapon to score many goals from outside the penalty area.

PRO TIPS

Try not to dawdle with the ball or be too obvious about where your pass is going to go. Play with your head up and try to make accurate passes to avoid the risk of interception.

The greater your range of passes, the more options you will have when you have the ball. Choosing when to use a particular pass is even more crucial. Think safety first when playing the ball out of your defensive third of the field and never consider it to be a failure if you choose to pass sideways or back when attacking. Keeping possession of the ball is important.

The back of your cleat can be used to strike through the middle of the ball. A back heel pass can reverse the direction of play and surprise opponents, but you must know that a teammate will be there to get the ball.

"Some teams can't or don't pass the ball. What are you playing for? What's the point?"

Xavi, Spain and Barcelona midfielder

CROSS: a pass sent from a wide position into the penalty area

Soccer terms

Heading

Around one in five goals is scored with a header, but heading isn't just used when attacking. It is a vital part of defensive play, and with the ball bouncing high off firm ground, headers can be used all over the field and by every player. Even goalkeepers use headers to clear a high ball when they are outside of their penalty area.

Headers are often directed downward, toward a teammate's feet or aimed at the goal. In these cases, players try to get their head over the ball and aim to connect just above the middle of the ball. When you want elevation on the ball—for example, to clear the ball up and over opponents—aim for just below the middle of the ball.

Get into line with the direction of the ball, watch it carefully, and spring upward, swinging your arms forward to help you leap up high.

A defensive header sees the player leap above an opponent. Strike the ball with your forehead but aim for the bottom half of the ball to clear it with height and power.

Rising above the ball, this attacker has managed to direct his header downward toward the bottom corner of the goal, making it very hard for the goalkeeper to react in time.

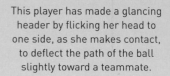

This player has made a glancing header by flicking her head to one side, as she makes contact, to deflect the path of the ball slightly toward a teammate.

Watch the ball until it is on your head and meet the ball with a forward thrust of your upper body and head. Aim to make contact with the middle of your forehead.

Keep your neck muscles firm as you connect to push the ball strongly away. Bend your knees to help cushion your landing.

The diving header is one of the most spectacular of all moves in soccer. This player has launched himself to get to the ball ahead of defenders and has glanced it toward the goal.

★ *Masterclass* ★

Tim Cahill

Tim Cahill times his jump to head the ball perfectly. Relatively short for a professional soccer player, at 5 ft. 10 in. (1.78m), the Australian midfielder is a masterful header of the ball both in defense and in attack. His bravery and powerful spring usually ensure that he gets to the ball ahead of his opponents.

PENALTY AREA: the rectangular area surrounding each goal

Soccer terms

Finding space

Space gives players the time and the opportunity to control the ball and develop their team's attack. Pockets of space appear all over the field, and good players learn to spot the most useful spaces to move into. Moving into these spaces can overstretch the other team or create an overload—an area of the field where the attacking team has more players than the defending team.

These attackers (in white) are playing a one-two move. The first attacker (the player closest to us) plays a short pass to his teammate, before sprinting quickly into space behind the defender in order to receive a return pass.

Moving into space is not just a question of spotting a promising free area of the field, but also of timing your move. Try to stay aware of where the ball and other players are and look to time your run to stay onside (see page 48). As soon as you make a pass, make sure that you move right away and look for another good position in order to receive the ball.

Timing your run to move toward the ball in space behind defense is an especially good move. One player makes an overlapping run outside a defender and along the edge of the field. His teammate plays the ball in front of him so that he can run onto it, behind the opposition's defense.

The attacker on the right has spotted her teammate making a well-timed diagonal run into space. With an accurate pass, she can send the ball over the opposition player so that her teammate is behind the defense.

Getting into space often means getting free from an opponent marking you. You should never jog aimlessly from place to place. Instead, make your runs sharp, accurate, and decisive. You can use changes of pace to get free from your marker as well as feints, in which you drop your shoulder and pretend to head one way, before pushing off hard from one foot and sprinting in a different direction.

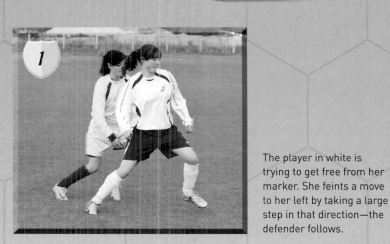

The player in white is trying to get free from her marker. She feints a move to her left by taking a large step in that direction—the defender follows.

As soon as she plants her left foot, she uses it to push off and move quickly to her right. The defender has been caught out by this move and has been left behind.

PRO TIPS

If you make a run into space but do not receive the ball and the game moves on, do not dawdle. Instead, look for other places to move into as soon as you can.

★ Masterclass ★

Xavi

Playing with his head up as usual, the talented Spanish midfielder is a master at seeking out space both to move into in order to receive a pass and to aim passes for teammates. Xavi made more passes than any player at the 2010 World Cup (669 in total) and is a crucial part of what makes his team, Barcelona, one of the most successful teams in the world.

Playing small-sided games and drills that emphasize quick passing and movement will help improve your ability to play with your head up, as well as to spot space and move into it quickly and decisively.

Soccer terms **FEINT**: using a fake move of the body to send an opponent in the wrong direction

Shielding and dribbling

The ball will often arrive when an opponent is very close to you. You can protect possession by getting your body between the opponent and the ball. This technique is called shielding. Running with the ball under close control is known as dribbling. It can be a useful technique for beating defenders when you are attacking.

Dribbling carries the risk of losing the ball, so it is best to use it as an attacking move only when a good pass is not available. Try to use both feet to nudge and push the ball, keeping it a little ahead of you, but not too far. In order for dribbling to be successful during a game, it should be performed quickly or with sudden changes of pace and direction.

Deception, fakes, and swerves are all part of becoming a successful dribbler. This dribbler (in white) fakes a move to her right, which the defender follows.

The defender lunges in the direction that she believes the dribbler is heading. At the same time, the dribbler brings her left foot around the ball to move it to her left.

With the ball under control, the dribbler moves sharply away to her left. The defender is unbalanced and unable to regain a good defensive position before the dribbler passes her.

When shielding the ball, you should be aware of where your opponent is at all times. Stay on the balls of your feet so that you can move as your opponent moves and keep your body and arms out to make as big a shield as possible. Keep the ball under control and think about your next move, whether this is a sharp turn or a pass to a teammate.

You can stand your ground as you shield the ball, but if you back into your opponent or cause an obstruction, then you commit a foul.

★ Masterclass ★

Lionel Messi

Argentinian maestro Lionel Messi shields the ball from the Greek defender Sokratis Papastathopoulos, during a 2010 World Cup game. Messi is relatively small and light, but with excellent balance, awareness, ball control, and movement, he is able to keep possession of the ball and dribble skillfully past defenders.

If you cannot turn past a defender, keep the ball shielded and look for a short pass to a teammate to the side of or behind you.

To complete a stepover, bring one foot across the ball as if it were to connect with the ball.

Instead of connecting, lift your foot over the ball and plant it to one side.

You can then use your other foot to tap the ball in the other direction, confusing a defender.

Alternatively, you can perform another stepover with the other foot.

A player works on his close control skills by dribbling through a slalom of poles with the ball under close control. A good way to learn many new moves is to attempt them at a walking pace first and to gradually build up speed as you improve.

In training

While you should practice your individual skills whenever you can, training sessions are where you can practice with others under the eye of your coach. He or she can give you direct tuition on key techniques while you work with teammates in fun and challenging drills and games and learn set-piece plays, such as special corner-kick or free-kick moves.

A coach works with players, showing the defenders good positions to take up when defending a corner. Good coaches organize varied and interesting sessions with different drills and games to challenge you and improve your skills.

Attending regular soccer training sessions will improve your physical fitness and stamina and allow you to practice passing, moving, attacking, and defending techniques with other players in realistic game situations. Working on your core individual skills in between training sessions will help improve your technique and ability rapidly.

Training can be thirsty work, so make sure you take small, regular sips from a water bottle during breaks in training.

Approach training as you would approach a game, by warming up and stretching thoroughly and then committing yourself to every part of the training session. Concentrate on each drill and always listen to your coach. If you do not understand a point, ask your coach to explain it to you.

This attacker is practicing his shooting while the goalkeeper is practicing his diving saves.

Games played in a small field area help improve your close control and decision making while under pressure. Here, players play a simple two-on-two game, where each team tries to keep possession of the ball for as long as possible, while their opponents try to win the ball by making tackles and intercepting passes.

This player is practicing shooting the ball while on the move. The ball is passed toward her, she runs toward it and aims for the corners of the goal between the posts and the cones.

Soccer terms   **SET PIECE:** a restart move such as a free kick, corner kick, or throw-in

Volleys and swerves

A volley is a strike of the ball while it is in the air. It can be powerful if it is performed well, but it is one of the trickiest skills to master. Softer volleys can be made to cushion a short pass to a teammate or to steer the ball into an open goal to score.

To make a side volley, lean away from the ball a little as you move your arms out and swing your leg up and around at the hip.

To make a front-on volley, swing your kicking leg back and then forward, holding out your arms for balance.

Keeping your head over the ball, point your foot down before striking the ball with your instep.

Swing your leg to follow through in the direction of the target.

Get your foot over the ball so that your instep makes contact with its top half, if you want to keep the ball down, or just below the middle if you are making a defensive clearance.

Volleys are used when there is little time to get the ball down and control it. This occurs both in attack and defense when you need to make a fast clearance. The secret with all volleys is to watch the ball carefully and to time your leg swing with the incoming ball's speed and direction.

To make an overhead kick, jump back off one leg and swing your other leg up and over to strike the ball with your instep at the highest point. Try to relax as you fall and roll onto your shoulders to absorb the impact.

"Make sure your nonkicking foot is firmly planted. If it isn't, you could be off-balance."

Alfred Galustian, technical adviser to the English Premier League

As you follow through, aim to get your foot on the ground and regain your balance as quickly as possible.

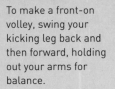

To strike an inside swerve with your right foot, plant your left foot away from the ball. Use the inside of your foot to strike the right-hand side of the back of the ball. Aim for a straight follow through of your leg to send the ball curving to the left.

★ Masterclass ★

Samir Nasri

This dynamic French midfielder is a master at bending the ball, either to hit a curling pass to a teammate or to unleash an incredible, swerving shot at the goal. After playing more than 120 times for the French team Marseille, Nasri enjoyed three seasons at Arsenal before moving to Manchester City for $40 million.

Hitting across the back and one side of the ball with a specific part of your cleat can put spin on the ball, making it swerve through the air. This can be useful not just to bend the ball around a defensive wall during a free kick, but also to cross the ball into the penalty area on a path curving toward or away from the goal.

Remember that swerving the ball along the sideline may get it past an opponent, but if the entire ball crosses the sideline while in the air, the other team will get a throw-in.

PRO TIPS

To hit an outside swerve, use the outside of your right cleat to strike across the back and left side of the ball. Your kicking foot should swing up and across your body as the ball curves to the right.

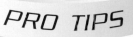

SWERVE: to bend the path of the ball

Soccer terms

An attacking team will aim to get a player into a position from which they can score. Sometimes, a burst of individual excellence can result in a goal. However, goals are usually a team effort, with players working together to create space for teammates or to release another attacker with a through ball behind the defense.

1

The player with the ball faces a crowded penalty area. His teammates aim to make diagonal attacking runs, staying onside until the ball is played.

2

The attacker to the left makes a run to one side, bringing his defender with him and creating space for the attacker on the ball to play a through ball into the gap.

Attacking

Good teams and players try to use all parts of the field to launch and develop attacks. By passing the ball from the center of the field and out wide, for example, you can aim to cross the ball into the penalty area. This can stretch the opposing team's defense, potentially creating gaps for players to run into.

You can sometimes beat an opponent without dribbling by pushing the ball past them and sprinting hard to get the ball back under control. This can work best along the sidelines when there is no marking defender nearby.

3

The other attacker can then run behind his marker into the space to receive the pass and shoot at the goal.

Mesut Özil

Mesut Özil plays a defense-splitting pass during Germany's 4–0 win against Australia at the 2010 World Cup. Özil is an exciting young attacking midfielder with a great eye for through balls, pinpoint crosses from wide positions, or sudden bursts through opposing defenses. After starring at the World Cup, Özil moved from Werder Bremen to Spanish team Real Madrid.

★ *Masterclass* ★

This attacker has run toward the goal after a teammate has shot. As a result, she is in a great position to pounce on a mistake by the goalkeeper and tap the ball into the net.

The attacker with the ball has spotted plenty of space behind the opposition's defense. He can play the ball diagonally across the field for his teammate on the far side to run toward.

THROUGH BALL: a pass made to a teammate behind the other team's defense

Soccer terms

Scoring goals

Scoring goals is great but also takes great skill. It requires sharp reactions, cool decision making, and sharp awareness of the game going on around you. While strikers may get more chances to score on average, all outfield players should work on their shooting, because defenders and midfielders often get opportunities to score during close games.

Different situations demand different types of shots, but try not to overhit the ball, even with longer-distance strikes to the goal, and make sure that your shot is on target. Work hard to perfect your shooting with both feet. This will give you more opportunity to strike and also stops a defender from forcing you onto your weaker foot.

Faced with just the goalkeeper, you can try to dribble around the player, strike a shot before the goalkeeper advances toward you, or, as this player has done, play an accurate chip, sending the ball over the diving goalkeeper and toward the goal.

★ Masterclass ★

Birgit Prinz
Birgit Prinz celebrates scoring a goal for her team, Frankfurt F.F.C. The German goal machine has scored more than 120 times for her country, more than 200 times for her team, and is the all-time leading scorer at the Women's World Cup, with 14 goals. She has also been FIFA World Player of the Year three times.

This player's first attempt at the goal rebounded off a defender, but by following up his own shot quickly, he gets to the ball first. Close to the goal, he opts for placement over power by making a sidefoot pass into the net.

If you are in a good shooting position, within your shooting range, and have a clear sight of the goal, do not hesitate—shoot! Soccer is a fast-moving sport, and within a second, defenders will close you down. Pick the type of shot you want to make, aim away from the goalkeeper, and try to keep your body over the ball to keep the shot low.

There are a lot of different drills you can use to work on your shooting skills. Here, one player controls the ball with her back to the goal.

Quick reactions and awareness close to the goal can make all the difference. The player on the left could shoot the ball to the goalkeeper's left or play to a teammate who is in a better position to score.

Once the ball is under control, she must turn quickly and fire off an accurate shot past the goalkeeper.

OUTFIELD PLAYER: any soccer player in a team except the goalkeeper

Soccer terms

Defending

Defending is a task for every player on a team, not just the goalkeeper and defenders. A well-organized team, with all players working hard for each other, denies the opposing team time and space to build up good attacks. When defending, you have two aims—to prevent goal-scoring chances being created and to regain possession of the ball for your team.

Defending begins from the front, with this attacker (in white) chasing down and harassing a defender with the ball. Pressure such as this can lead to a defender making a mistake and your team regaining the ball.

In some teams, each defender is instructed by their coach to guard an area of the field—a technique known as zonal marking. Most junior teams prefer man-marking, in which each defender and some midfielders are responsible for staying close to a particular opponent. They stay close as their opponents move in order to deny them time and space to receive the ball.

This marker (in yellow) stays sharp and moves as his opponent moves, staying on the balls of his feet so he can move quickly in any direction. He stays goalside of his opponent at all times.

As an opponent shoots, the defender gets his body and legs in the way to block the ball. When you block a shot, try to keep your hands close to your body to avoid a handball offense.

This defender has jockeyed his opponent, delaying his movement toward the goal as a teammate arrives to provide defensive cover. Once his teammate is in support, the defender may choose to challenge for the ball.

Jockeying is the skill of closing down an opponent and delaying their progress in an attack. Get into a good, defensive stance around 3–7 ft. (1–2m) in front of your opponent, with your knees bent and eyes on the ball and try to keep your distance by retreating in a zigzag pattern. If you can, try to direct your opponent away from the goal.

This defender (in yellow) is under pressure from two attackers. She has no choice but to put the ball out of play over the sideline, giving her time to get back into position.

Clearing the ball can relieve pressure on your team. If you have time with the ball, aim to make an accurate pass to a teammate in plenty of space. If time is short, aim to strike the ball upfield.

> *"Stay on your feet, don't dive in—defending is all about timing."*
>
> Rio Ferdinand, Manchester United and England defender

Soccer terms | **GOALSIDE:** placing your body in between the goal and the ball or an opponent

Challenging for the ball

The aim of challenging for the ball is to win back possession for your team. This might not always be possible, but any challenge should at least try to slow down an opponent's attack. An ideal challenge sees you move away with the ball under your control, ready to turn defense into attack.

This defender has used his pace to get ahead of an opponent with the ball. Shoulder charging an opponent is illegal, but some contact between the players' shoulders is acceptable.

★ Masterclass ★

Maicon

Brazilian defender Maicon times a sliding tackle perfectly to dispossess U.S.A. midfielder DaMarcus Beasley. Strong and decisive when challenging for the ball, Maicon looks to regain possession and turn defense into attack whenever possible. A superb defender for his team, Inter Milan, he was voted UEFA Club Defender of the Year in 2010.

Try to make a challenge when you have teammates providing cover between you and your goal. Sometimes, a defender can race in and intercept the ball without tackling. If you have to make a challenge, try to stay on your feet and make sure that you connect with the ball rather than your opponent.

1

The defender (in yellow) aims to make a front block tackle. She establishes a firm low base with a strong stance and her standing leg bent slightly at the knee. Her eyes watch the ball rather than the player as she times her challenge.

2

She uses the inside of her cleat to make a strong strike through the middle of the ball, leaning into the challenge as the impact occurs. With all of her body weight in the tackle, the ball spills free, and she reacts quickly to get it under control.

Shielding player is static, with too wide of a stance

Defender pokes ball away with the toe of his cleat

Block tackles see you put your body weight into a firm strike of the ball with the inside of your foot. The ball can sometimes get wedged between your foot and your opponent's. In this situation, the first to flick or roll the ball up and over the other's foot often gains possession of the ball.

When an opponent shields the ball from you, look for opportunities to win possession, pressure your opponent into a mistake, or move the ball out of your opponent's control—but be careful not to give away a foul. This defender has managed to poke his foot between the attacker's legs and nudge away the ball.

A block tackle can be made from the side using a similar technique to the front block. Time your approach, face your opponent, and bend your standing leg at the knee before striking the ball firmly with the inside of your cleat.

Goalkeeping

Good goalkeeping is as much about awareness and positioning as about spectacular saves. As a goalkeeper, you are your team's defensive leader. You are responsible for organizing the team during set pieces, such as corner kicks and free kicks, and when an opposing team breaks with the ball. You should also pass on advice and instructions to teammates, making them clear and loud.

Goalkeeping starts from the ready position, where you are balanced with your weight equally on the balls of both feet and your knees slightly bent. From this position, you can move easily and quickly in any direction, reacting to move in line with the ball to block a shot, jump quickly toward a deflection, collect the ball in cleanly, or sprint forward to kick the ball clear.

This goalkeeper is in a good ready position, with his hands up and out, his head level, and his eyes focused on the ball and play ahead of him.

Stay alert for a back pass from a teammate. If headed back, you can catch the ball, but if it is kicked, you cannot pick it up. If under pressure, think safety first and kick the ball out of play.

PRO TIPS

To collect a ball rolling along or just above the ground, get in line with the ball's path, drop down onto one knee, and scoop the ball up to your chest. Your leg and body act as a barrier behind your hands.

To catch a high ball, leap up from one foot and stretch up with your arms. Aim to catch it in front of you, spreading your hands around the back and sides of the ball.

Overarm throws are used
to roll the ball out quickly
over medium to long
distances. With a wide,
side-on stance for balance,
bring your throwing arm
forward over your head
and release the ball. Your
other arm should point
to your intended target.

★ Masterclass ★

Gianluigi Buffon

The Italian goalkeeper keeps his
eye on the ball as he stretches to
deflect a shot around his post. Buffon
became the world's most expensive
goalkeeper when he transferred from
Parma to Juventus for $52 million in
2001. His calmness under pressure
and expert positioning allow him
to stop many attacks.

If you think you cannot
catch a high ball cleanly
you can punch it clear
with two hands. Aim to
punch through the back
of the ball to send it
forward and up, out of
your penalty area.

To roll the ball out accurately over
shorter distances, get down low
with your front foot pointing to your
target. Roll the ball out with a firm
underarm motion.

To catch a ball around waist height, scoop the ball
into your body. Cushion its arrival by bending and
folding your body around the ball.

To perform a drop kick, hold the ball
out in front of you, drop it, and aim to
hit the ball—just before it reaches the
ground—with the instep of your cleat.

Advanced goalkeeping

Sometimes, good positioning is not enough and an opposing attacker bursts through to the goal. These are the moments when a goalkeeper needs bravery, explosive agility, and good technique to make a crucial save. In these situations, goalkeepers must be quick and decisive. If they fail to get to the ball first and collide with or trip an attacker, they will give away a penalty and may be shown a red card.

Diving at the feet of an opponent can be a scary experience, so practice it gently in training to build up your confidence. In a game situation, once you decide to go to ground, attack the ball. Keep your eyes on the ball, not the opponent, and try to spread yourself, creating a long barrier across the ground. Get your hands on the ball and wrap your body around it for added protection.

If you spot the flight of a shot heading to one side of you, you may be forced to make a diving save. Try to take short, very quick steps in that direction and start bending the knee closest to that side.

Transfer your body weight over your bent knee and push off hard from that foot to spring up and across your goal. Keep your eyes on the ball and the path that it is traveling in.

With a goalkeeper staying on his line, an attacker with the ball has the entire goal to aim at. The goalkeeper will struggle if an attacker makes a shot into the corners.

Narrowing the angle is a key positioning technique to reduce the amount of the goal an opponent with the ball can shoot at. You need to come out of your goal but stay positioned along an imaginary line running from the ball to the center of your goal.

PRO TIPS

All goalkeepers have a stronger and weaker side and saves that they prefer. Work hard on your weaker side and least-favorite saves to bring them up to the level of your other skills.

This goalkeeper has come off his line to narrow the angle and has spread his body and arms to look as big as possible. Attackers can see much less of the goal, and, as a result, they may hit a shot that is too wide.

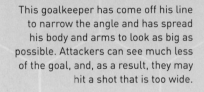

As you dive, stretch both of your arms out and a little in front of you, so you can watch the ball right into your hands. Your hands should be nicely spread but close enough together to be ready to grasp the sides and back of the ball.

With the ball caught, collect it into your body and prepare for landing. Try to land on your side, using it as a buffer or cushion when you hit the ground to stop the ball from jarring out of your grip.

Soccer terms | **RED CARD**: shown by a referee to send a player off the field

Laws of the game

The rules of soccer are enforced on the field by the referee and two assistants, who communicate with the referee using flag signals. The referee must decide whether a foul has been committed and judge which team touched the ball last when awarding corner kicks, throw-ins, and goal kicks. Never argue with a referee's call—the referee's decision is final.

Referees can discipline individual players by showing a yellow card for a range of offenses, including fouls, arguing with the referee, or preventing the restart of play. More severe offenses result in a red card. In this case, the offending player leaves the field and his or her team must continue with one fewer player.

The attacker (in white) has been fouled by his opponent but has managed to keep hold of the ball and is in a good attacking position. Instead of stopping play and awarding a free kick, the referee lets the attacker continue and puts both of his arms out in front to signal that he is playing advantage.

With his team in the lead, this goalkeeper has held on to the ball for longer than ten seconds. He is guilty of delaying the restart of play—known as timewasting—and the referee cautions him by showing a yellow card. If a player is shown two yellow cards during a game, then he or she is automatically shown a red card and must leave the field.

Pretending to be fouled is known as simulation. In this case, the referee is playing advantage as the diving player has not been fouled. He can also award a free kick to the opposition.

Throw-in

Substitution being made

Offside

A player is offside if, as the ball is played by a teammate, they are closer to the opposition's goal line than both the ball and the second-to-last opponent. You cannot be offside if you receive the ball directly from a throw-in, corner kick, or goal kick. If you are offside, the referee will award an indirect free kick to the other team.

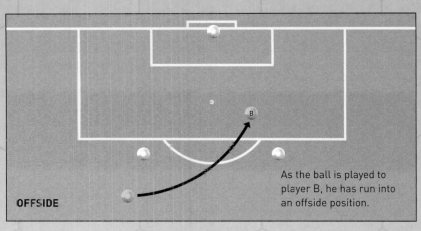

OFFSIDE

As the ball is played to player B, he has run into an offside position.

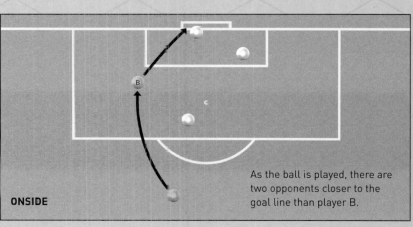

ONSIDE

As the ball is played, there are two opponents closer to the goal line than player B.

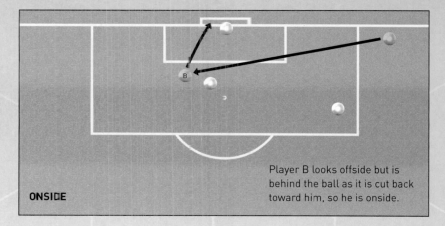

ONSIDE

Player B looks offside but is behind the ball as it is cut back toward him, so he is onside.

Penalty

Indirect free kick

Red card

Corner kick

Goal kick

Soccer terms **ADVANTAGE:** when a referee lets play continue after a law has been broken

Throw-ins are given when the ball crosses the field's sideline. A player must keep two hands on the ball during the throw, and his or her feet must be on or behind the sideline. To make a longer throw, you can take several steps to build momentum before launching the ball. Arch your back and whip your arms and body forward, releasing the ball with a flick of your fingers.

For a throw-in, pull your arms back over your head with your hands spread around the back and sides of the ball and keep both feet on the ground.

Whip your upper body forward as your arms travel over your head. Release the ball with a flick of your wrists and fingers to help direct the ball.

This player commits a foul throw because he has stepped over the sideline. Other causes of a foul throw are lifting one foot off the ground and not bringing the ball back over your head.

Restarting play

Play stops for a number of reasons—for example, if the ball goes out of bounds across a goal line or sideline or if the referee halts the game for an injury or foul. The game is restarted in several ways. These are great opportunities for your team to build up attacks. For this reason, moves involving corner kicks and throw-ins are often part of training for a team.

Successful throw-ins rely on cooperation between teammates in order to secure possession. Here, this throw-in decoy move sees one teammate sprint toward the thrower, drawing the defender with him. This creates space behind for the other attacker to run into and receive the ball from the throw.

Most corner kicks are aimed at the front of the goal area for attackers to try to head at the goal. The corner-kick taker must beat the first defender, who is often placed in front of the closer goalpost. Good corner-kick takers aim to put plenty of pace on the ball, as the slightest deflection can propel the ball toward the goal.

By bending the ball (see page 27), you can send the ball curving away from the goal (an out-swinging corner) or in toward the goal (an in-swinging corner). Both can be dangerous. An out-swinger curves away from the goalkeeper and toward attackers running into the penalty area.

Corner kicks are given when the ball goes out of bounds from either end of the field and the defending team touched it last. The ball has to be placed inside the corner arc, and opponents must retreat at least 30 ft. (9.1m). The corner-kick taker has plenty of options, including passing the ball along the ground to a teammate making a run to the front of the penalty area or hitting a high cross deep into the goal area.

Successful corner kicks rely on both a good delivery and well-timed runs by attackers into the penalty area. Here, two attackers on the right are timing their runs into the box to meet the corner at just the right time. Another option is to play a short corner kick to the edge of the penalty area to catch out the other team.

Drop balls are used to restart the game after some stoppages. The referee stands between one player from each team and releases the ball. The players can challenge for the ball as soon as it touches the ground.

Soccer terms **FIRST DEFENDER:** the defender closest to the corner kick, who is usually placed on the closer goalpost

Fouls and free kicks

There is usually some physical contact during a game of soccer. However, when one team gains an unfair advantage by breaking a law, such as being caught offside, the referee will stop play by blowing his or her whistle and award a free kick to the opposing team.

Referees award two types of free kicks—indirect and direct. A goalkeeper handling a backpass or a player causing dangerous play will result in an indirect free kick. Here, the ball must be touched by one player before a second player can shoot at the goal. A direct free kick can be shot at the goal and is awarded for fouls such as pushing, tripping, or kicking an opponent.

This player has used an unfair amount of force to barge his opponent out of the way and almost send him sprawling to the ground. The referee will stop the game to award a free kick to the fouled player's team at the place where the offense occurred.

Some contact during a tackle is often inevitable, but if the player connects with an opponent before playing the ball, then the referee will signal a foul.

A player who deliberately handles the ball or sticks out an arm to block its path is guilty of a handball. The referee will award a free kick.

Tugging the shirt of an opponent to prevent their movement or laying your hands on an opponent's body to pull or hold them back are fouls.

Awarded a free kick, this alert player places the ball and is looking for opportunities to take a quick free kick. He can pass forward to a teammate and start an attack before the other team can regroup.

The referee and assistants try to get every decision correct, but they will not always be in the best position to judge a split second of action. Always accept the officials' decisions and never argue. Instead, retreat rapidly into a good defensive position in case your opponents take a quick free kick.

As soon as a free kick is given against your team, retreat to at least 30 ft. (9.1m) from the ball. If you fail to do so, the referee may show you a yellow card.

★ *Masterclass* ★

Cristiano Ronaldo

With his incredible pace and trickery, Portuguese winger Cristiano Ronaldo often lures opponents into giving away free kicks for fouls. He is also an expert at taking them. Thousands of hours of practice have given Ronaldo an array of free-kick shots, including fiercely struck shots that bend and dip on their way to the goal.

An attacking free kick usually sees a defensive wall of players positioned to guard most of the goal. The free-kick taker may aim to bend the ball up and over or around the edge of the wall toward the goal. Alternatively, he or she may choose to pass the ball to one side, bypassing the wall, for a teammate to have a clear strike at the goal.

Soccer terms   **WALL:** a row of defenders protecting their goal against a free kick

Penalties

A foul or infringement by the defending team inside of their penalty area, such as a deliberate handball, will see the referee award a penalty kick. This is a superb chance to score, with the ball placed just 36 ft. (11.1m) from the goal and only the goalkeeper to beat. Even so, many penalties are missed because of poor technique or an outstanding save.

A goalkeeper stands on the balls of his feet, ready to spring as the penalty kick is taken. A goalkeeper can move along his or her goal line before the kick is taken but must not move forward.

A defender has badly fouled and brought down an attacker who was about to shoot inside the penalty area. The referee awards a penalty to the attacking team and may show the defender a red card.

Taking a penalty is an exercise in staying calm and using good technique. Decide on the type of penalty you want to take before your run-up and stick to it. Make sure that you get your body over the ball and strike it through the middle— this will help keep the ball down and on target.

Carefully place the ball on the penalty spot, treading down on any divots around the ball, and pace out your run-up. Try to shut out all distractions and focus on where you intend to aim the ball.

This penalty-kick taker has used a firm sidefoot pass for control and aimed the ball into one of the corners—difficult for any goalkeeper to reach. Other players choose to kick the ball with an instep drive for power.

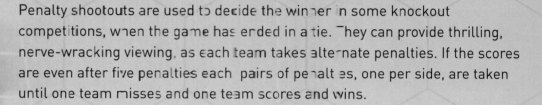

Penalty shootouts are used to decide the winner in some knockout competitions, when the game has ended in a tie. They can provide thrilling, nerve-wracking viewing, as each team takes alternate penalties. If the scores are even after five penalties each pairs of penalties, one per side, are taken until one team misses and one team scores and wins.

Stay alert and do not turn away in disgust if your penalty is saved. The goalkeeper may push the ball back out, giving you a second shot at the goal.

⚽ **PRO TIPS** ⚽

This goalkeeper has chosen the right direction to dive and makes a save. In a regular penalty kick, players can follow up, so the goalkeeper will want to hold onto the ball. In a penalty shootout, no opponent can follow up with a second attempt at the goal.

Players from both teams must stay outside of the penalty area until the ball has been struck. They can then race into the area to either clear a rebound, if they are on the defending side, or to try to score if they are on the attacking team.

RUN-UP: the paces that a player takes as he or she moves toward the ball to take a shot

Soccer terms

Team tactics

Tactics are the way in which a team plays during a game—how the players try to defend and attack, where they are positioned, and their specific roles. A coach is in charge of tactics and will aim to catch out an opposing team by exploiting weaknesses such as slow or inexperienced full-backs or using his or her own team's strengths to their fullest.

Even with the same formations, two teams can play quite differently by adopting different styles of play. Some teams use long, upfield passes to their strikers to launch quick attacks, while others prefer more patient build-up play, using a lot of short passes to keep possession and push for openings.

Teams line up at the start of a game in rows of defenders, midfielders, and attackers. This is called a formation. This 4-4-2 formation features two strikers playing in front of four midfielders.

4-4-2 formation

A team's defenders have moved up quickly and decisively in a straight line across the field to catch an opponent offside. This offside trap is used as a defensive tactic by some teams.

A single striker may be played upfront, using strength and skill to shield the ball and make layoff passes to fellow attackers who play a short distance behind them.

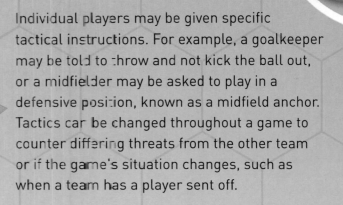

3-5-2 formation

This is a popular formation, as it can be set out as attack-minded or defensive. The wide midfielders in a 3-5-2 formation can push on when their team has the ball to provide a lot of width in an attack.

Individual players may be given specific tactical instructions. For example, a goalkeeper may be told to throw and not kick the ball out, or a midfielder may be asked to play in a defensive position, known as a midfield anchor. Tactics can be changed throughout a game to counter differing threats from the other team or if the game's situation changes, such as when a team has a player sent off.

4-4-1-1 formation

Popular with many teams, 4-4-1-1 sees four defenders and midfielders aiming to feed a center forward with a second striker playing in the hole behind him or her.

An attacker is substituted for a midfielder by a team's coach. Substitutions are a vital part of tactical play, allowing a coach to replace a tired or underperforming player or to reshape the team to be more attack- or defense-minded.

Sometimes, a team may choose one of its midfielders to mark a dangerous opponent, such as a playmaker who often sets up chances for strikers. The aim is to starve the player of time and space in which to create chances.

Read about soccer tactics and watch the analysis of games on TV to learn more about how teams play. If you are unsure of a tactic your team is adopting, always ask your coach to explain it.

PRO TIPS

SUBSTITUTION: replacing one player on the team with another from the substitutes' bench

Soccer terms

Young players train at Ajax's Academy. The Dutch team's youth system is famous for producing many talented players, including Edwin van der Sar, Johan Cruyff, Rafael van der Vaart, and Wesley Sneijder.

Professional soccer

All talented young soccer players dream of being paid to play for a professional team. As they progress through school, local, and regional teams, young players may be signed to train and hone their skills in a professional team's youth system. Competition is fierce, and only a tiny handful of young players will ever make the cut.

Supporters of the Brazilian team Flamengo make a colorful spectacle during a game against Boa Vista. All over the world, fans flock to watch their team play, devoting a lot of time and money to follow them.

Soccer is played at professional level by teams on every continent, but the powerhouse leagues containing the world's richest teams are all found in Europe. These attract the cream of playing talent from Africa, Asia, and the Americas, giving many top European teams a truly international flavor.

An English Premier League game really is an international affair. Here, Everton's English midfielder, Leon Osman, is crowded out by three Manchester City players—Ivorian Yaya Touré, Vincent Kompany from Belgium, and Samir Nasri from France.

At its top end, professional soccer is a massive business. In 2011, for example, Real Madrid earned more than $600 million, while Barcelona pay Lionel Messi over $42 million per season. Top players are wealthy and major celebrities, but fame and fortune dwindle rapidly outside the biggest leagues, with some teams struggling to stay in business.

Professional soccer leagues exist for women in a number of countries, including Germany, North America (the Women's Professional Soccer league), and, from 2011, England (the Women's Super League). Here, Shannon Boxx (left) of the Los Angeles Sol and Yael Averbuch of the New Jersey Sky Blue chase the ball during a WPS game.

Cristiano Ronaldo and Kaka attack for Real Madrid, the team that broke the world transfer record to sign Kaka for $89 million in 2007 and again in 2009 to sign Ronaldo for $128 million.

A selection of jerseys, scarves, and other merchandise go on sale at a Chelsea F.C. stall. Sales of merchandise and tickets, along with sponsorship and the sale of TV rights, are key ways in which soccer teams make money.

"My interest is in the collective success of the team, not individual glory."

Lionel Messi, Barcelona and Argentina player

MERCHANDISE: souvenirs, clothing, and other items bought by fans

Major competitions

Soccer teams compete in leagues (where teams play each other twice or more in a season) and knockout cup competitions both within their own country and involving teams from overseas. These include the Copa Libertadores in South America and the UEFA Champions League in Europe.

El Hadji Diouf, playing for Glasgow Rangers, evades the challenge of Celtic's Beran Kayal (right) during their 2011 Scottish Cup clash. Celtic and Rangers are the competition's most successful teams, winning the trophy 34 and 33 times, respectively.

The Japanese J League began as a professional competition in 1993 and now features 18 teams. The Kashima Antlers is its most successful team, with seven league titles.

Two giants of European soccer, Inter Milan and Bayern Munich, compete in a 2010–2011 UEFA Champions League game. These two teams have reached the final of the competition (or the European Cup it replaced) a total of 13 times.

National teams also take part in continental competitions. These include the UEFA European Championship and the Asian Cup. The oldest continental competition, the Copa America for South American teams, began in 1916. The African Cup of Nations started out with just three teams in 1957, but now more than 50 take part. Countries also send men's and women's teams to compete in the Summer Olympics.

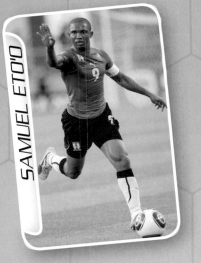

SAMUEL ETO'O

Cameroon's star striker, Samuel Eto'o is the African Cup of Nations' record goalscorer, with 18 goals in six tournaments.

Leyton Orient, three league divisions below Arsenal, battle to a 1-1 tie in a 2011 FA Cup game. First held all the way back in 1871–1872, the FA Cup is the oldest-surviving cup competition in the world.

LDU Quito plays the Uruguayan team Penarol in the 2011 Copa Libertadores. Three years earlier, LDU Quito became the first team from Ecuador to win the competition.

Australia's Brett Holman (right) challenges Iraq's Qusai Munir during the 2011 Asian Cup. Australia began competing in Asian soccer in 2007, the same year that Iraq won the competition.

Egypt's players celebrate winning their third African Cup of Nations in a row in 2010. They are the competition's most successful team, with seven wins.

The World Cup

Since its launch in 1930, the peak of soccer competition is the FIFA World Cup. Players in more than 200 national teams dream of qualifying for the 32-team tournament, which is held once every four years. Teams that reach the World Cup finals know that they are just seven games away from lifting the famous trophy as world champions.

SOUTH AFRICA

Iker Casillas holds the World Cup trophy in the air as his Spanish teammates celebrate winning the 2010 World Cup in front of more than 84,000 spectators.

South African fans cheer on their team during the 2010 World Cup. The tournament was held in their country and was the first time it had been hosted in Africa.

Brazilian players celebrate scoring against Scotland during a "friendly" game. Brazil will host the 2014 World Cup, with the final to be played in Rio de Janeiro.

Teams battle it out in qualifying competitions in their region to reach the finals. They are then split into eight groups, each with four teams. The top two teams in each group go into a knockout competition. The next three rounds of games determine the two teams that will play in the final. Brazil is the most successful nation, winning five times; Italy has four wins, and Germany has three. The German team has also finished in the top three at the tournament a record 11 times.

Germany's Linda Bresonik defends against Argentina during a record-breaking 2007 Women's World Cup game that Germany won 11–0.

The FIFA Women's World Cup began in 1991 and has greatly helped boost the profile of women's soccer. The U.S.A., Norway, Japan, and Germany have all won the competition, while China, Brazil, and Sweden have all reached the final.

Diego Forlán controls the bouncing ball, shielding it from South Korean opponents during the 2010 World Cup. With five goals, Forlán was awarded the Golden Ball as the tournament's best player.

With just four minutes of extra time remaining, Andrés Iniesta shoots past Maarten Stekelenburg to win the 2010 World Cup for Spain, which came with a $30 million winners' prize.

Soccer terms **EXTRA TIME:** a period of extra play in some competitions when the scores are even after full time

Soccer legends

Throughout soccer's history, certain players have amazed and dazzled with their skills, athleticism, and daring. Here are some of the game's greatest legends and current leading stars.

Franz Beckenbauer

A superb defender for Bayern Munich and West Germany, Beckenbauer revolutionized the role of sweeper to stride into midfield and build attacks. He scored 14 times for his country, captained them to World Cup glory in 1974, and coached them to victory in the 1990 finals.

Lionel Messi

The talented Argentinian attacker has spent all of his adult career at Barcelona, where he has dazzled fans with mazy dribbling and extraordinary goals. He is currently considered the best attacking player on the planet.

Michel Platini

Part of a talented French team of the late 1970s and 1980s, Platini was an excellent passer and a spectacular free-kick taker who scored regularly. Since 2007, he has been president of UEFA, the body that runs soccer in Europe.

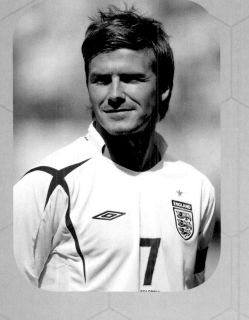

David Beckham

Beckham spent ten years at Manchester United, where his accurate passes and free-kick taking prowess helped the team to six Premier League titles and the 1999 UEFA Champions League. A move to Real Madrid was followed by a transfer to LA Galaxy in 2007.

Hakan Sükür

This Turkish striker played three stints with Galatasaray and scored more than 350 times for various teams. His 51 goals for the Turkish national team include the World Cup's fastest ever, scored after just 10.89 seconds, when Turkey finished third at the 2006 World Cup.

Marta

Small, at only 5 ft. 4 in. (1.63m) in height, yet packing a powerful shot, the Brazilian forward has been named World Player of the Year a record five times.

Lev Yashin

This goalkeeping great enjoyed more than 20 years at Dinamo Moscow, from 1949 to 1971, and played for the Soviet Union 78 times. The Lev Yashin Award is now given to the best goalkeeper at each World Cup.

George Best

Wayward but amazing, George Best had stints with more than a dozen teams but is best known for his barnstorming displays for Manchester United. Capable of riding brutal tackles and swerving and dribbling through an entire defense, Best entertained millions of fans.

SWEEPER: a defender who plays behind the main line of defenders

Soccer terms

Iker Casillas

One of the finest goalkeepers of the modern era, Casillas has played all of his adult soccer for Real Madrid. Casillas is known for his agility, and in 2010 he was judged to be the best goalkeeper at the World Cup, which Spain won.

Ferenc Puskas

Packing a powerful shot, Puskas was the jewel in the crown of a Hungarian team that won the 1952 Olympics and crushed opponents with their attacking play. He won three European Cups with Real Madrid.

Pelé

Arguably the greatest soccer player of all time, Pelé was certainly the game's finest all-around attacker, scoring 77 goals for Brazil and more than 1,200 for Santos and his other teams. The only player to win three World Cup winner's medals, Pelé remains a much-loved and respected figure in international soccer.

Cristiano Ronaldo

With blistering pace and tremendous skill, Ronaldo is a modern soccer superstar. He moved from Manchester United to Real Madrid in 2009 and has continued scoring at a rate of more than 20 goals per season.

Eusébio

African soccer's first superstar, Eusébio moved from his native Mozambique to play for Benfica in 1960. He scored more than 450 goals for the team and was the top scorer at the 1966 World Cup with nine.

Birgit Prinz

A powerful player and lethal goalscorer, Prinz was the youngest player ever to appear in a World Cup final in 1995. She has since played more than 200 times for Germany.

Diego Maradona

The only realistic rival to Pelé's crown as the best soccer player, the stocky Argentinian was simply impossible to stop at times. He scored FIFA's goal of the century—a 200-ft. (60-m) dribble past many of the England team at the 1986 World Cup.

Gheorghe Hagi

Unpredictable and highly skillful, Gheorghe Hagi was Romania's finest player in the 1980s and 1990s, winning 125 caps and scoring 34 goals for his country. After stints with teams including Real Madrid, Hagi helped the Turkish side Galatasaray win the 2000 UEFA Cup.

Soccer terms | **CAPS**: the number of appearances made by a soccer player for their national team

Johan Cruyff

A truly talented attacker, Cruyff scored 33 times in just 48 appearances for the Netherlands. Cruyff enjoyed great success at Ajax and Barcelona.

Zbigniew Boniek

The scorer of an awesome hat trick (three goals) against Belgium in the 1982 World Cup, in which Poland finished third, Boniek was a hard-running, attacking midfielder. After seven seasons at Widzew Lodz, he joined Michel Platini at Juventus, winning Serie A titles and the 1985 European Cup.

Xavi Hernández

A master at unlocking defenses, Xavi has spent his entire team career at Barcelona, where he has won six Spanish league titles and three Champions League crowns. Xavi has also won the 2008 European Championship and the 2010 World Cup with Spain.

Zinedine Zidane

Zidane played a key role as France swept to World Cup glory in 1998 and then became Euro 2000 champions. Sudden bursts of pace, a perfect first touch, and excellent awareness allowed him to get through defenses with attacking passes or runs. Zidane enjoyed stints at both Juventus and Real Madrid before retiring in 2006.

Kelly Smith

England's finest female soccer player, Kelly Smith's goals and pace helped propel Arsenal Ladies F.C. to four league titles and three women's FA Cups. She has also won more than 100 caps for her national team.

Hristo Stoichkov

Bulgaria's most famous player, Stoichkov had sudden acceleration and a blistering shot. He was adept at free kicks and scored 37 goals for his national team, who finished fourth at the 1994 World Cup.

Mia Hamm

One of the golden generation of American female players, Mia Hamm won World Cups and Olympic gold medals. She was the first female player to break the 100-goal international barrier in 1999, a testament to her ice-cool finishing and athletic, all-around play.

Landon Donovan

A Major League Soccer (MLS) superstar during his seasons at San Jose Earthquakes and LA Galaxy, Donovan has also played for Bayer Leverkusen and had short-loan stints with Bayern Munich and Everton. Making his debut for the U.S. team against Mexico in 2000, he has since become the U.S. team's leading scorer, with 45 goals.

Ronaldo

Starting his professional career with the Brazilian team Cruzeiro, Ronaldo moved to Europe, where he played for PSV Eindhoven, Barcelona, Inter Milan, and Real Madrid, as well as scoring more than 60 goals for Brazil. Ronaldo's tally of 15 World Cup goals is an all-time record.

Soccer terms   **SERIE A:** the top Italian league championship

Glossary

advantage
When a referee lets play continue after one of the laws of the game has been broken, giving the fouled-against team a benefit or advantage to continue an attack.

assistant referee
An official who assists the referee during the game, running up and down the sideline with a flag.

back heel
A short pass made with the back of the foot.

caps
The number of appearances made by a player for his or her national team.

chip pass
A pass lofted steeply into the air from a player to a teammate or as a shot at the goal.

cross
A pass sent from a wide position into the penalty area.

crossbar
The horizontal bar that connects the tops of the goal's two upright posts.

cushioning
Slowing down the path of the ball using a part of the body, such as the foot, chest, or head.

deflection
A sudden change in the direction of the ball after it has hit a player.

dribbling
Moving the ball under close control with a series of short kicks or taps.

extra time
A period of extra play in some competitions, when the scores are even after full time.

feint
Using a fake move of the body to send an opponent in the wrong direction or to put them off-balance.

FIFA
Short for Fédération Internationale de Football Association, the international governing body of soccer.

first defender
The defender closest to the corner kick, who is usually placed at the closest goalpost.

flexibility
The amount you can move your joints and body parts.

football
The term used for soccer in other parts of the world.

formation
The way in which a team lines up on the field in terms of defenders, midfielders, and forwards.

free kick
A kick awarded to a team when the opposition breaks one of the game's laws.

goalside
Placing your body in between the goal and the ball or an opponent.

instep
The part of a player's foot where their shoelaces lie.

intercepting
When one team makes a pass but an opponent gains control of the ball.

jockeying
A defensive technique of delaying an opposition player with the ball from passing or continuing an attack.

marking
Guarding a player to prevent him or her from advancing the ball toward the goal, making an easy pass, or getting the ball from a teammate.

merchandise
Souvenirs, clothing, game programs, and other items for sale, bought by fans.

obstruction
Blocking an opponent from reaching the ball without any attempt to reach the ball yourself.

opponent
A player from the other, opposing, soccer team.

overlap
To make a run beyond a teammate along the side of the field.

overload
A situation in which the attacking

team has more players in an area of the field than the defending team.

penalty area
The rectangular area, 132 ft. (40.2m) wide, surrounding each goal.

penalty kick
A kick awarded to a team when the opposition breaks one of the game's laws inside their own penalty area. Only the penalty-kick taker and the goalkeeper are allowed inside of the penalty area during the kick.

penalty shootout
A method of deciding a tied game by a series of penalties, taken from one end of the field.

possession
When one player or team has control of the ball.

professional
Soccer in which the players are paid a full-time salary to play.

red card
Shown by a referee to send a player off the field as a punishment for a serious offense.

Serie A
The top Italian league championship.

set piece
A planned play or move that a team uses when a game is restarted with a free kick, penalty kick, corner kick, goal kick, throw-in, or kickoff.

shielding
The technique of protecting the ball by placing your body between the ball and an opponent.

stamina
An athlete's ability to perform at or close to his or her peak performance for long periods.

substitution
Replacing one player on the team with another from the substitutes' bench.

sweeper
A defender who plays behind the main line of defenders, sweeping up any attacks that break through the defensive line.

swerve
To bend the path of the ball. A swerve is made by striking the ball with one side of the foot so that it spins in a certain direction.

tactics
Methods of play used in an attempt to outwit and beat an opposing team.

through ball
A pass made to a teammate behind the other team's defense.

UEFA
Short for Union of European Football Associations, the governing body of soccer (football) in Europe.

wall
A row of defenders protecting their goal against a free kick.

warmup
The routine of stretches and gentle exercises performed by players to prepare their bodies before training or a game.

yellow card
Shown by a referee to warn a player who has committed an offense.

zonal marking
When each defending player guards a particular area of the field.

Websites

http://soccernet.espn.go.com/index?cc=5739
ESPN's soccer website is full of information about the major cups, leagues, and international competitions all over the world.

http://usyouthsoccer.org/index2.html
The site of the U.S. Youth Soccer Association, featuring news about young players, competitions, and a calendar of events.

www.fifa.com/en/index.html
The official website of the organization that runs world soccer. The website contains details of qualifying and performances in leading tournaments, plus profiles of many leading teams and players.

www.premierleague.com
This official website of the English Premier League contains details of fixtures, results, and many features on teams and players.

www.uefa.com
The homepage of the Union of European Football Associations, the organization that runs the European Championship as well as the Champions League.

www.ussoccer.com
The official home of U.S. soccer in its many forms, including news and results from U.S. leagues and U.S. players overseas.

www.womensprosoccer.com
The official website of Women's Professional Soccer. It is packed with player and team profiles, as well as exciting photos and video clips.

Index

Picture credits

The Publisher would like to thank the following for permission to reproduce their material. Every care has been taken to trace copyright holders. However, if there have been unintentional omissions or failure to trace copyright holders, we apologize and will, if informed, endeavor to make corrections in any future edition.

t = top; b = bottom; c = center; l = left; r = right

6bl Bongarts/Getty Images, 6–7c Getty Images, 7bl Getty Images, 7tr AFP/Getty Images, 8 Getty Images, 15tr Getty Images, 17tr The FA via Getty Images, 19bl Bongarts/Getty Images, 19br AFP/Getty Images, 21br Getty Images, 23tr AFP/Getty Images, 26bl AFP/Getty Images, 27tr AFP/Getty Images, 29tr AFP/Getty Images, 30bl Bongarts/Getty Images, 34bl Bongarts/Getty Images, 37tl Getty Images, 44bl The FA via Getty Images, 45tr Getty Images, 50t Joachim Ladefoged/VII/Corbis, 50cr LatinContent/Getty Images, 50b AFP/Getty Images, 51tl Getty Images, 51bl Getty Images, 51r MLS via Getty Images, 52cl AFP/Getty Images, 52tr Getty Images, 52b Getty Images, 53tl AFP/Getty Images, 53tc Getty Images, 53tr AFP/Getty Images, 53b AFP/Getty Images, 53br AFP/Getty Images, 54cl AFP/Getty Images, 54b AFP/Getty Images, 54–55 Getty Images, 54–55b AFP/Getty Images, 55tr AFP/Getty Images, 55br 2010 Bob Thomas/Getty, 56bl Bob Thomas/Getty Images, 56r AFP/Getty Images, 57tl WireImage/ Getty Images, 57tr AFP/Getty Images, 57br Getty Images, 58tl AFP/Getty Images, 58tr AFP/Getty Images, 58b Time & Life Pictures/Getty Images, 59t Getty Images, 59cl Bongarts/Getty Images, 59cr Getty Images, 59b Bob Thomas/Getty Images, 60tl AFP/Getty Images, 60tr Bob Thomas/Getty Images, 60b AFP/Getty Images, 61l Getty Images, 61tr Bob Thomas/Getty Images, 61b AFP/Getty Images.